1 Number Puzzle 1 to 5 Butterfly

Name

Date

To parents
Write your child's name and the date in the boxes above. Teach your child the order of numbers from 1 to 5. Your child's lines may not be steady at first, but will improve with practice. Make sure to praise your child for his or her hard work.

■ Draw a line from 1 to 5 in order while saying each number.

Lemon

■Draw a line from 1 to 5 in order while saying each number.

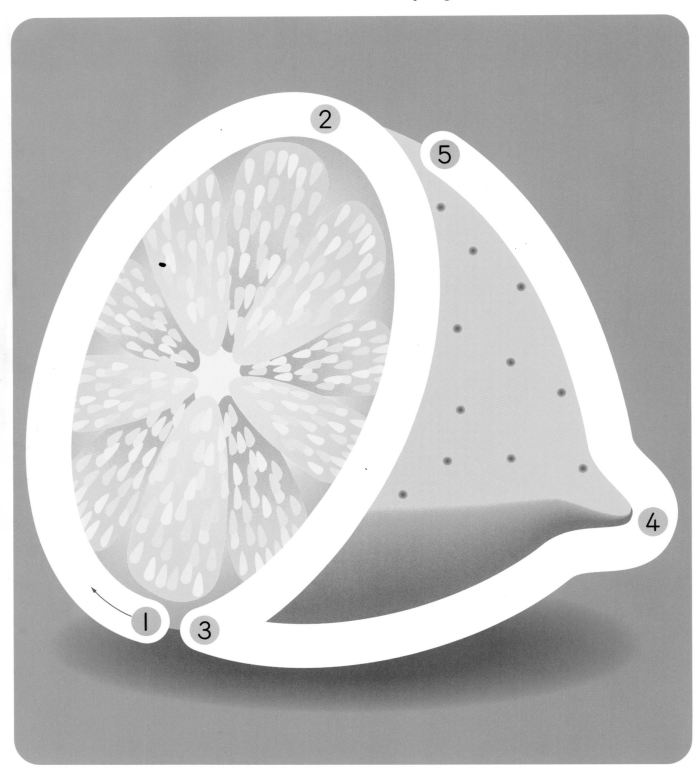

2 Counting 1 to 10

Name

Date

To parents
If it is difficult for your child to draw a line from 1 to 10 at
once, allow him or her to pause at each shell.

■Draw a line from 1 (●) to 10 (★) in order while saying each number.

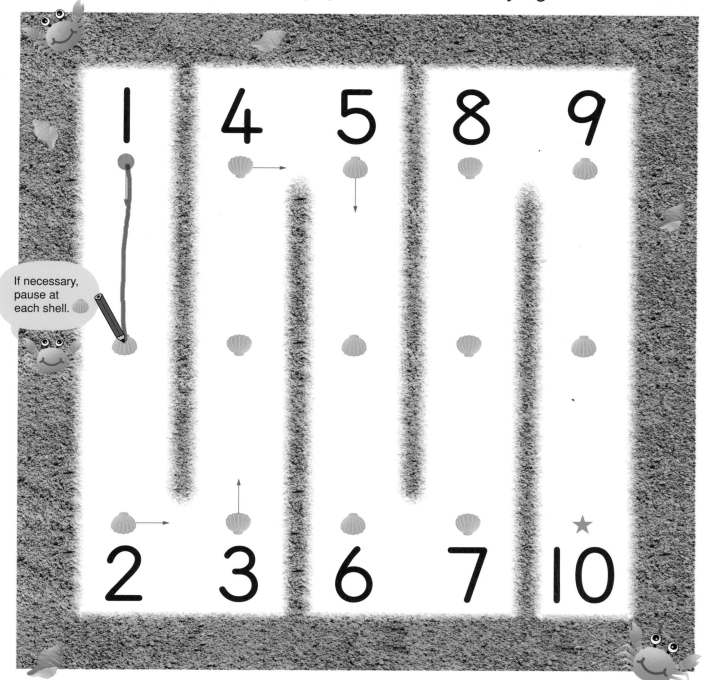

■Draw a line from 1 (●) to 10 (★) in order while saying each number.

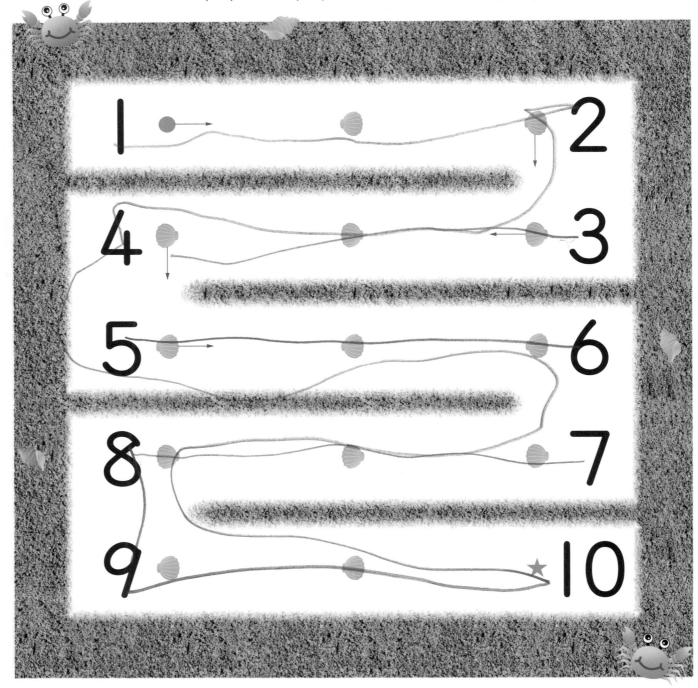

3 Number Puzzle 1 to 10
Cat

Name

Date

■ Draw a line from 1 to 10 in order while saying each number.

Dog

▪Draw a line from 1 to 10 in order while saying each number.

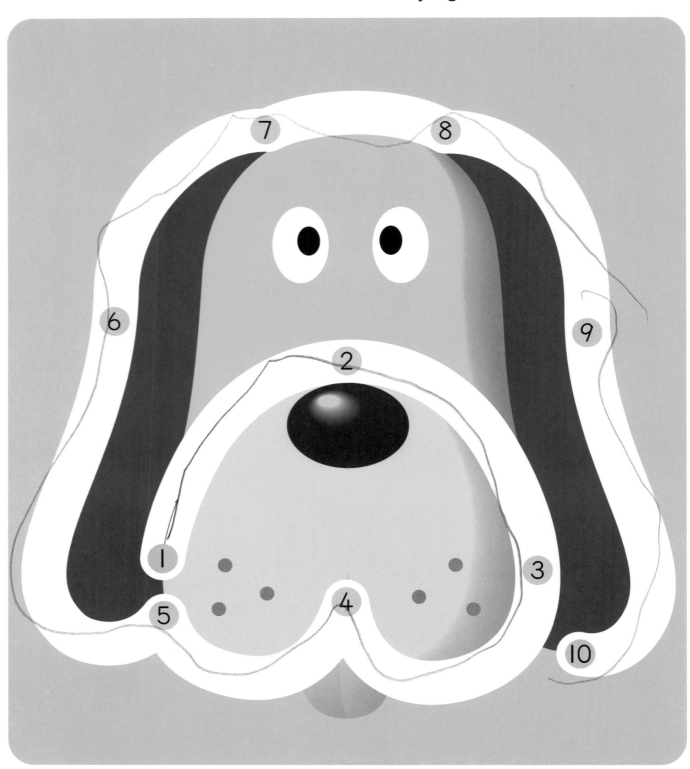

Number Puzzle 1 to 10
In the Sea

Name

Date

To parents
Have your child connect the dots from 1 to 10. This activity will help your child learn the order of numbers. If he or she doesn't know how to do this activity, point to the number 1 to show the starting point.

■ Draw a line from I (●) to I0 (★) in order while saying each number.

A Nice Day for Sailing

■Draw a line from I (●) to I0 (★) in order while saying each number.

Counting 1 to 10

Name

Date

To parents
Make sure that your child understands the order of the numbers. It helps to have your child trace first with his or her finger and then draw a line connecting the numbers.

■ Draw a line from 1 to 10 in order while saying each number.

■Draw a line from 1 to 10 in order while saying each number.

6 Writing Numbers 1 and 2

Name

Date

To parents
Have your child say the numbers aloud. Though the stroke path on this page is fairly wide, it may be challenging for your child to draw straight lines. It is important for your child to practice counting in daily activities. Find opportunities for him or her to have fun with numbers.

■Write the number I and say it aloud.

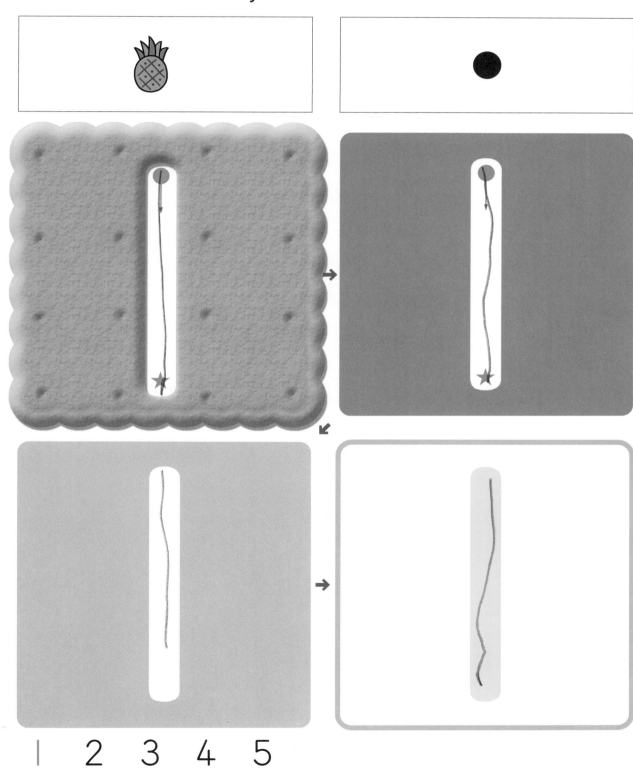

| 2 3 4 5

■Write the number 2 and say it aloud.

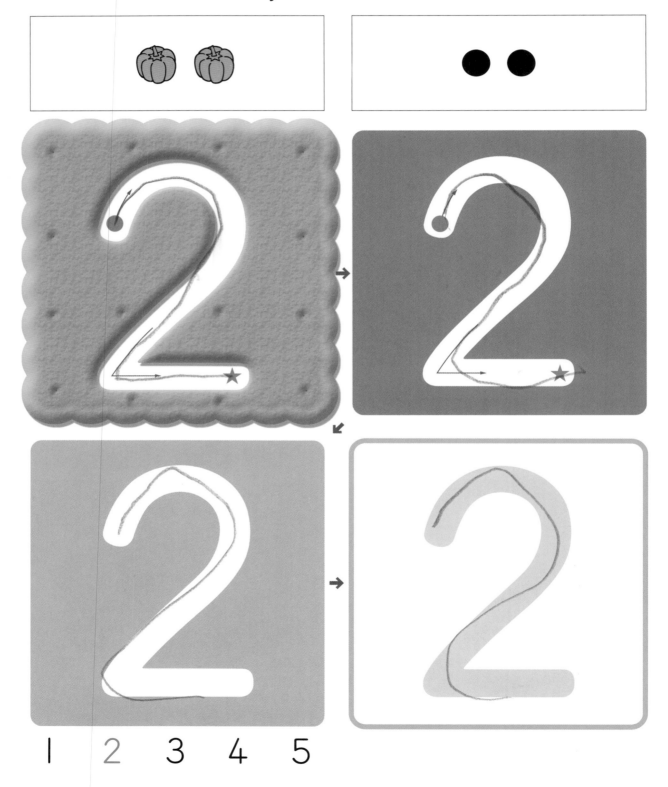

7 **Writing Numbers 3 and 4**

Name

Date

■ Write the number 3 and say it aloud.

1 2 3 4 5

To parents
First, demonstrate how to write the number 4 which is written in two strokes.
Guide your child's hand if necessary, then have him or her start writing from ①.

■ Write the number 4 and say it aloud.

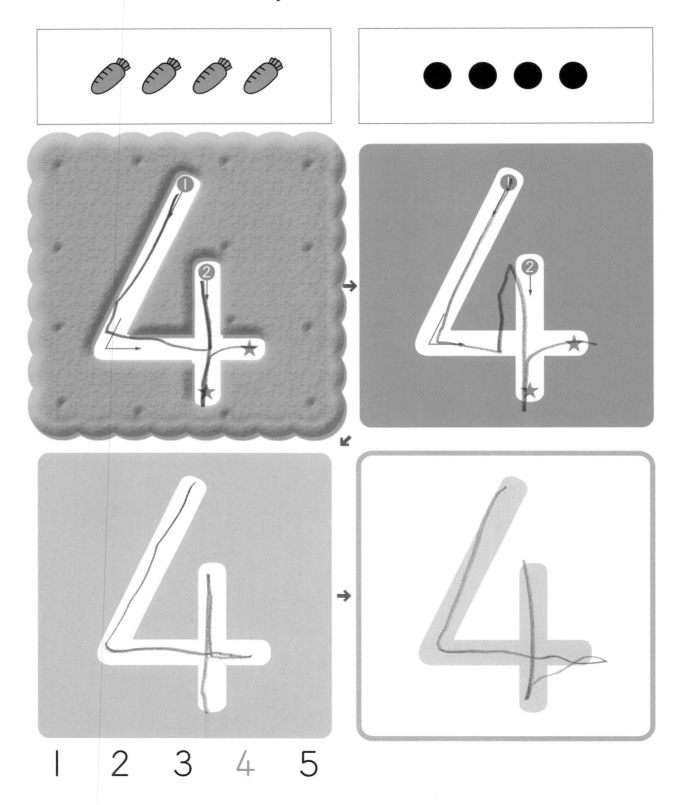

1   2   3   4   5

Writing Numbers 5 and 6

Name

Date

To parents
First, demonstrate how to write the number 5. Guide your child's hand if necessary, then have him or her start writing from ①.

■Write the number 5 and say it aloud.

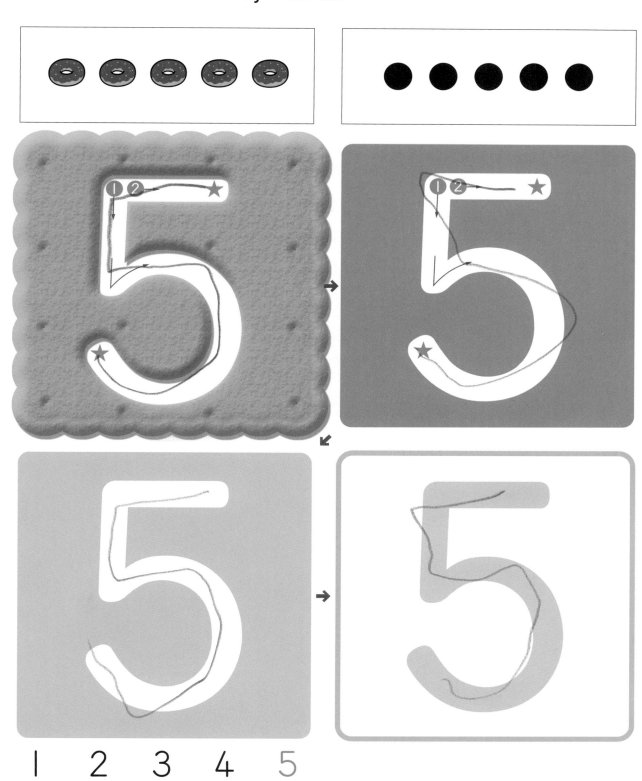

1　2　3　4　5

■Write the number 6 and say it aloud.

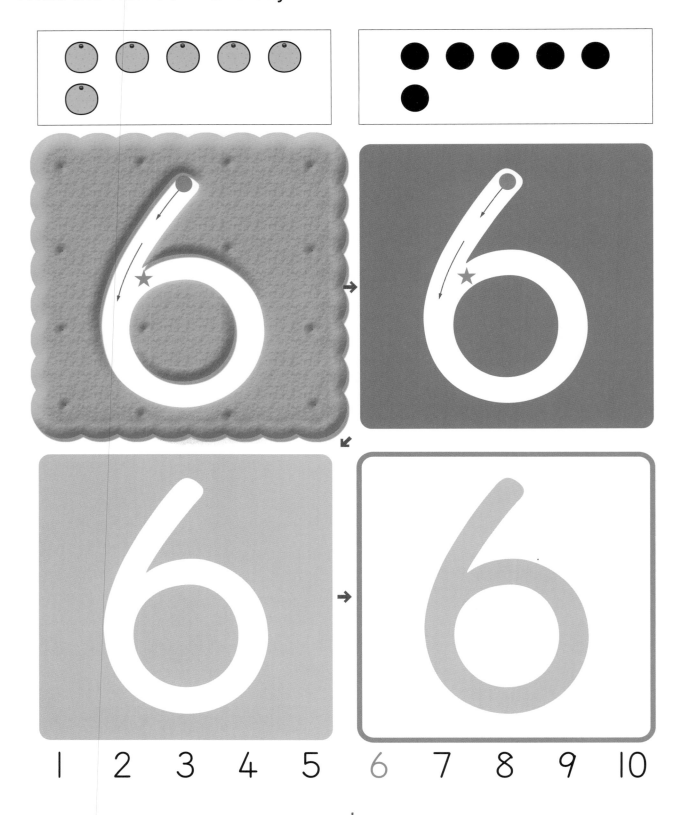

1 2 3 4 5 6 7 8 9 10

9 Writing Numbers 7 and 8

Name

Date

■ Write the number 7 and say it aloud.

| 1 | 2 | 3 | 4 | 5 | 6 | 7 | 8 | 9 | 10 |

■Write the number 8 and say it aloud.

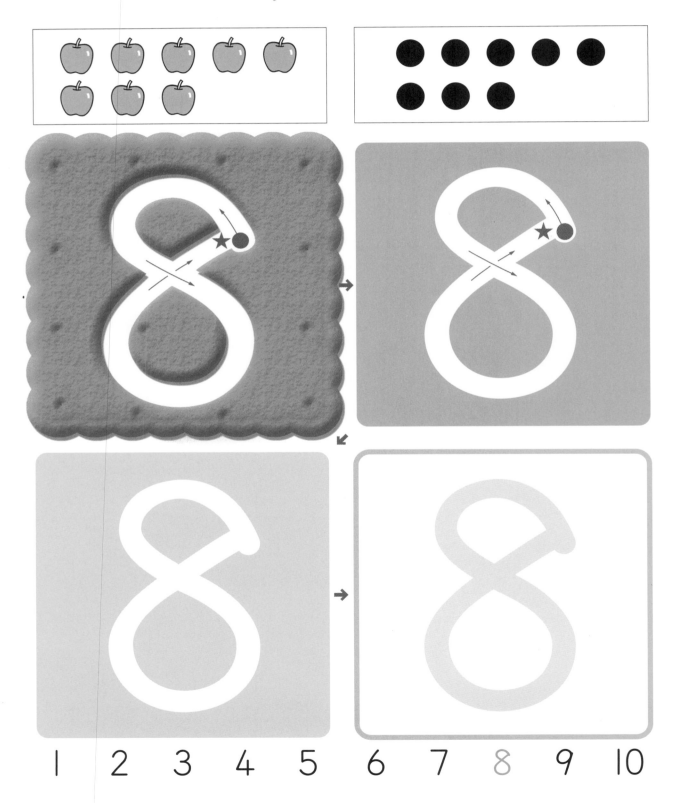

Writing Numbers 9 and 10

Name

Date

■ Write the number 9 and say it aloud.

1   2   3   4   5   6   7   8   9   10

■Write the number 10 and say it aloud.

Writing Numbers 1 to 4

Name

Date

To parents
Have your child write the numbers. Check that they are the proper size.

■ Write the numbers and say them aloud.

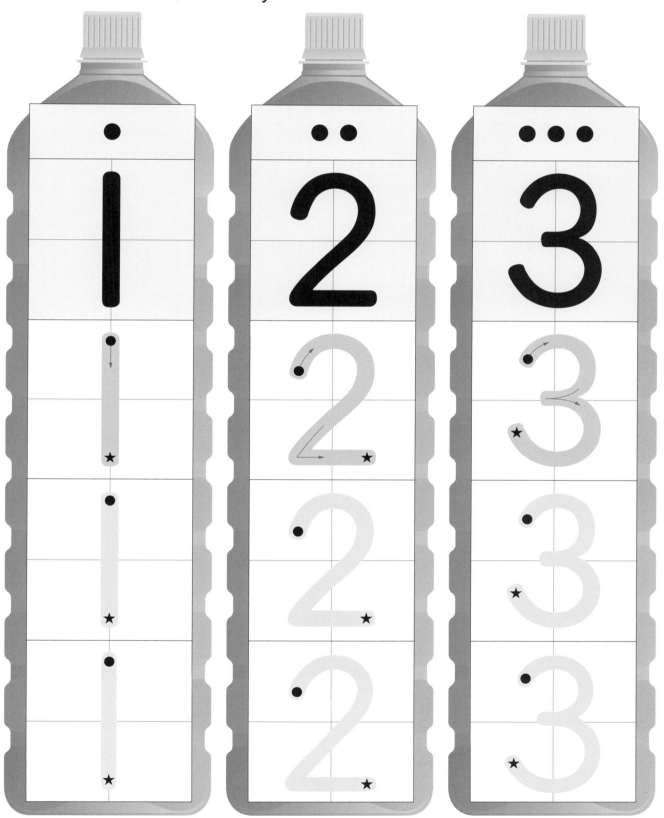

■Write the numbers and say them aloud.

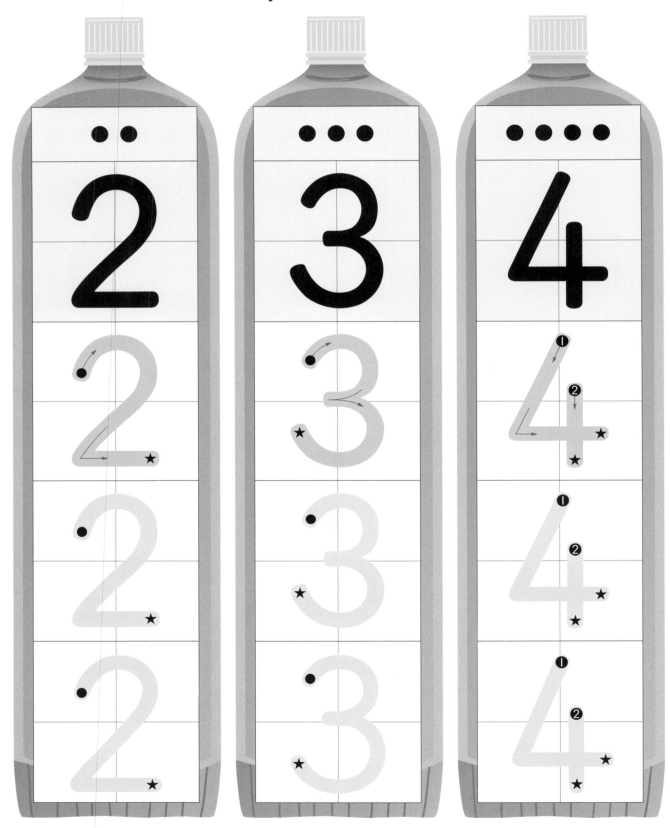

12 Writing Numbers 3 to 6

Name

Date

■Write the numbers and say them aloud.

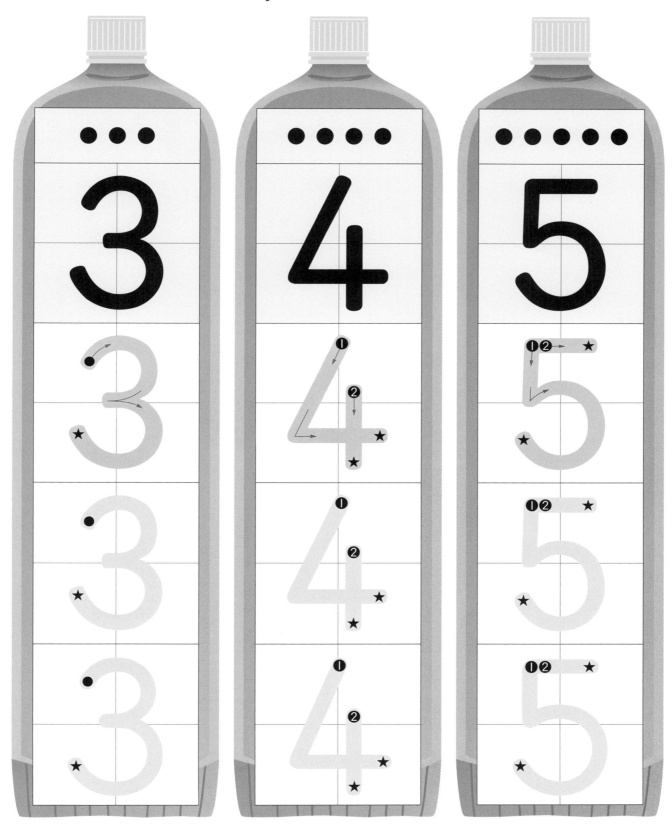

Write the numbers and say them aloud.

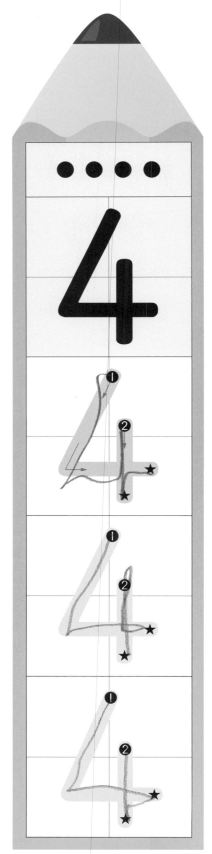

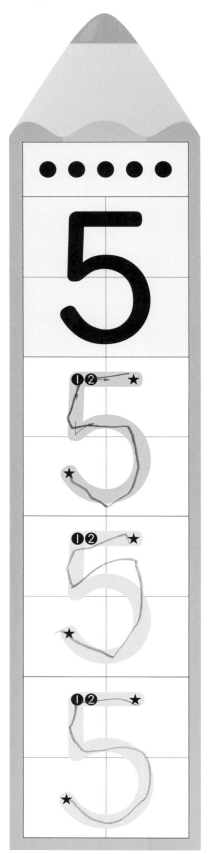

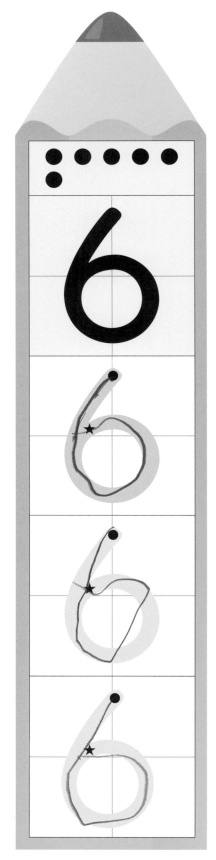

13 Writing Numbers 5 to 8

Name

Date

■ Write the numbers and say them aloud.

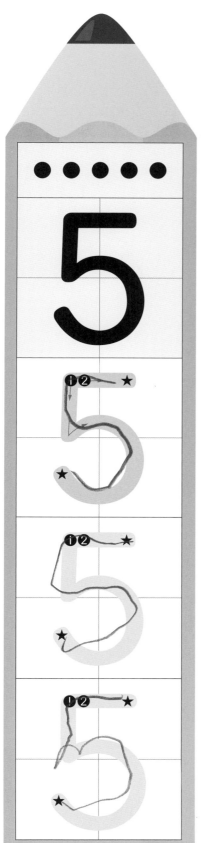

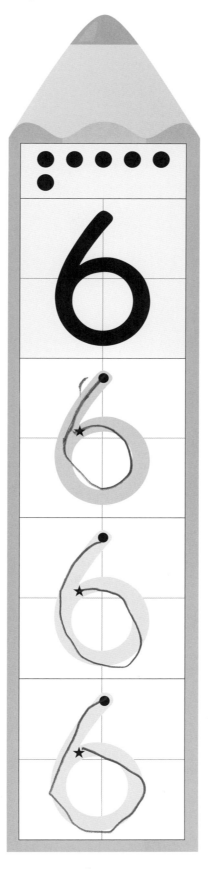

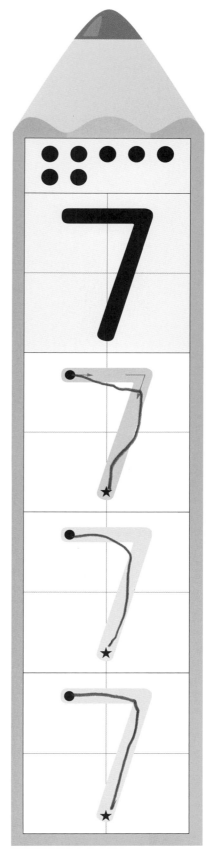

■Write the numbers and say them aloud.

6

7

8

Writing Numbers
7 to 10

Name

Date

■ Write the numbers and say them aloud.

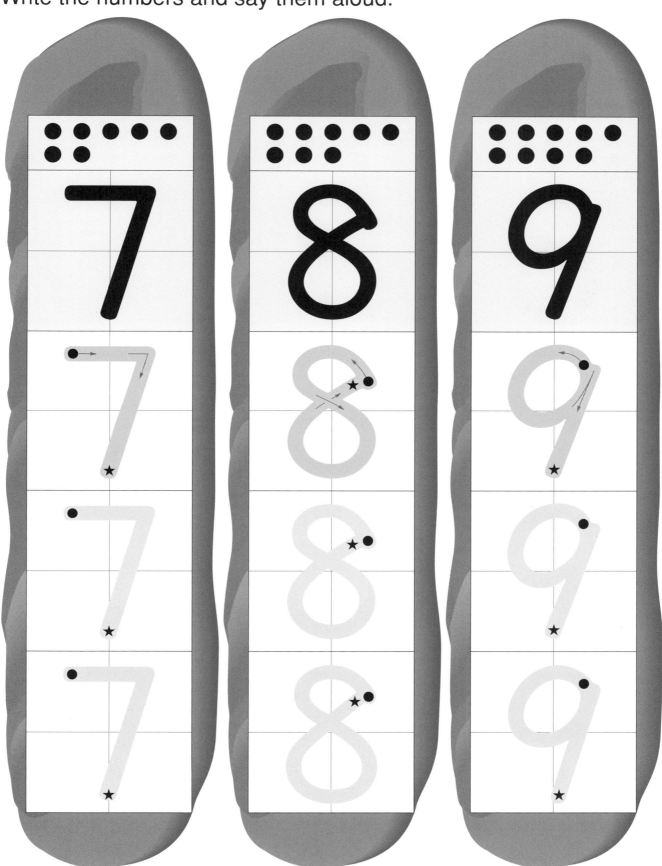

■Write the numbers and say them aloud.

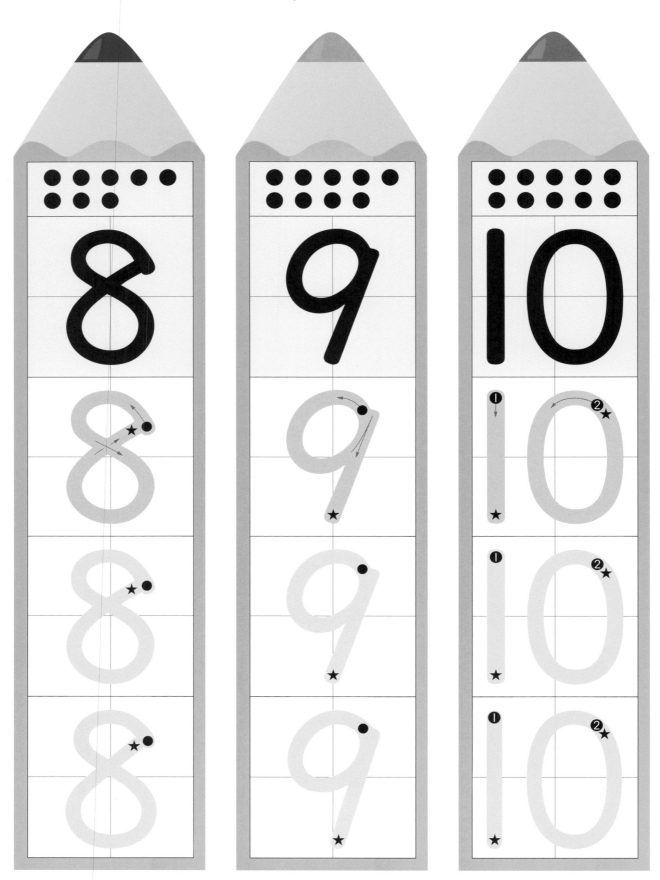

Writing Numbers 1 to 6

Name

Date

To parents
From this page on, the stroke path becomes narrower and no stroke order is shown. Make sure that your child writes the numbers 4 and 5 in the right stroke order.

▪ Write the numbers and say them aloud.

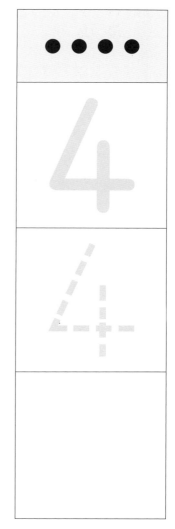

■Write the numbers and say them aloud.

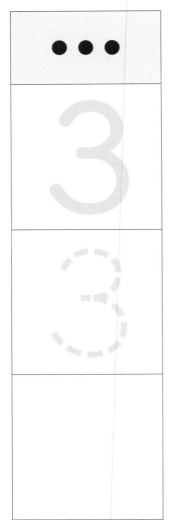

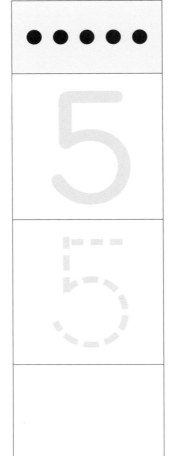

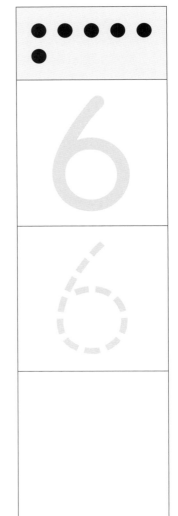

16 Writing Numbers 5 to 10

■ Write the numbers and say them aloud.

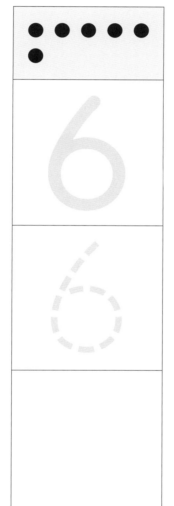

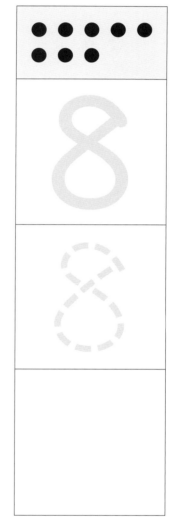

■Write the numbers and say them aloud.

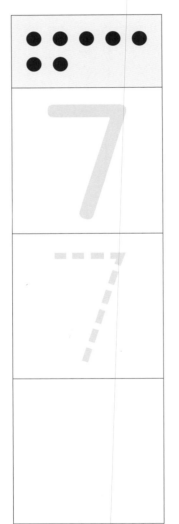 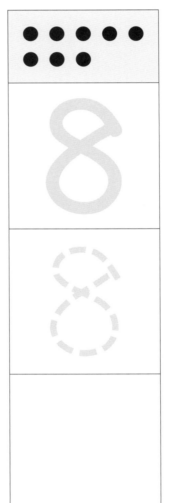  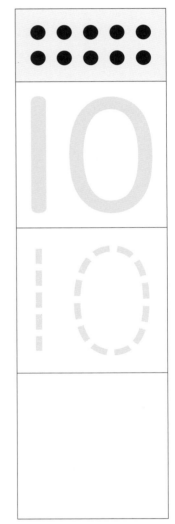

17 How Many? 1 to 5

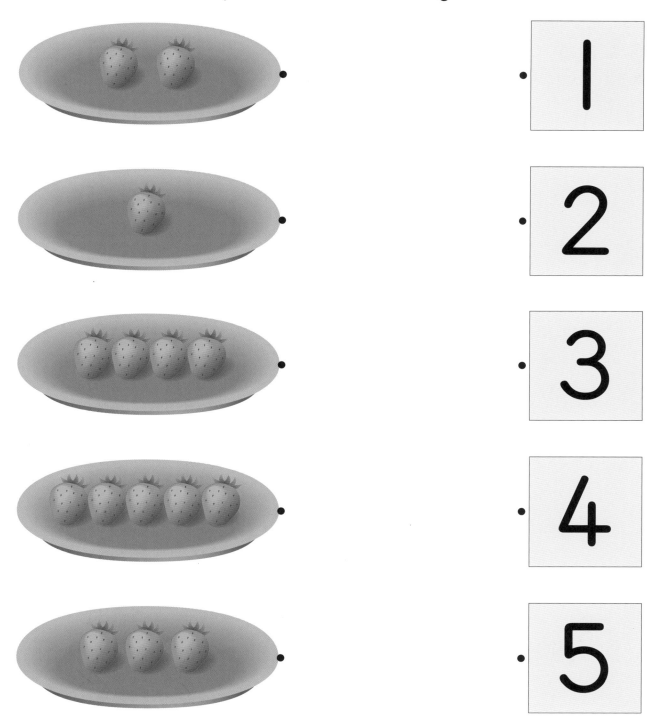

Name

Date

To parents
In addition to being a sequence, numbers also represent quantities. It is important for your child to practice counting in daily activities.

■ How many are there?
Draw a line from each picture to the matching number.

1

2

3

4

5

■How many are there?
  Draw a line from the dots (●) to the matching number.

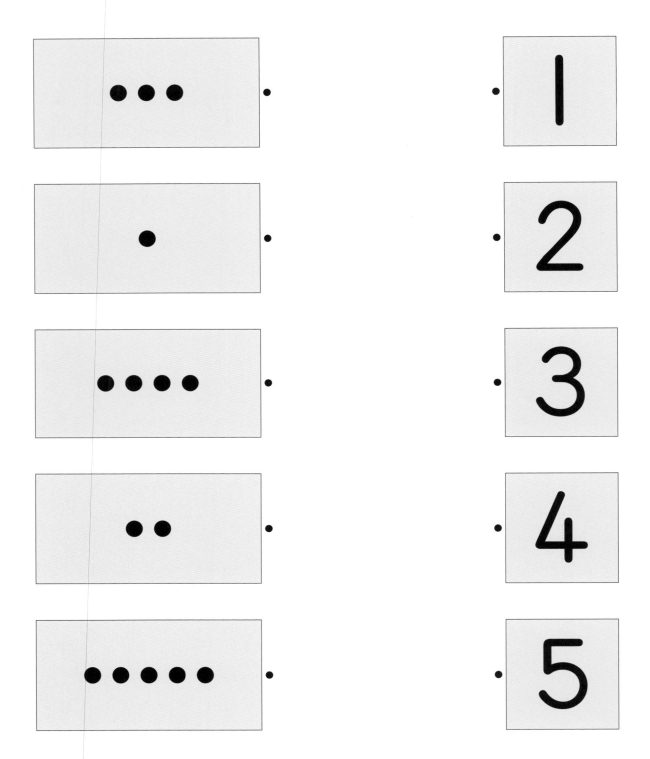

18 How Many? 6 to 10

Name

Date

■How many are there?
  Draw a line from each picture to the matching number.

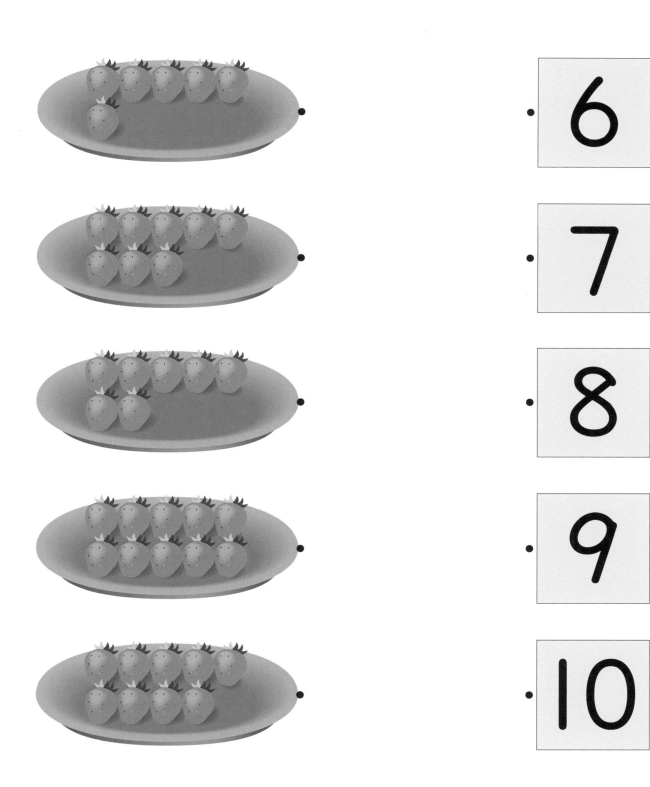

■How many are there?
Draw a line from the dots (●) to the matching number.

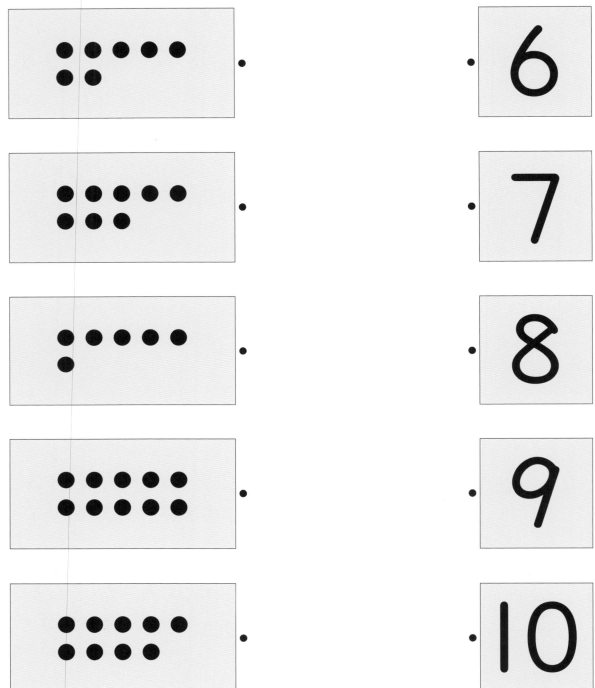

How Many? 1 to 10

To parents
First, have your child look at the objects and count them aloud. Then have him or her trace the numbers.

■How many are there? Trace the gray numbers.

🍍	🎃🎃	🍅🍅🍅	🥕🥕🥕🥕	🍩🍩🍩🍩🍩
1	**2**	**3**	**4**	**5**
1	2	3	4	5

🍊🍊🍊🍊🍊🍊	🧁🧁🧁🧁🧁🧁🧁	🍎🍎🍎🍎🍎🍎🍎🍎	🍓🍓🍓🍓🍓🍓🍓🍓🍓	🍬🍬🍬🍬🍬🍬🍬🍬🍬🍬
6	**7**	**8**	**9**	**10**
6	7	8	9	10

How many are there?
Trace the gray numbers and fill in the empty boxes.

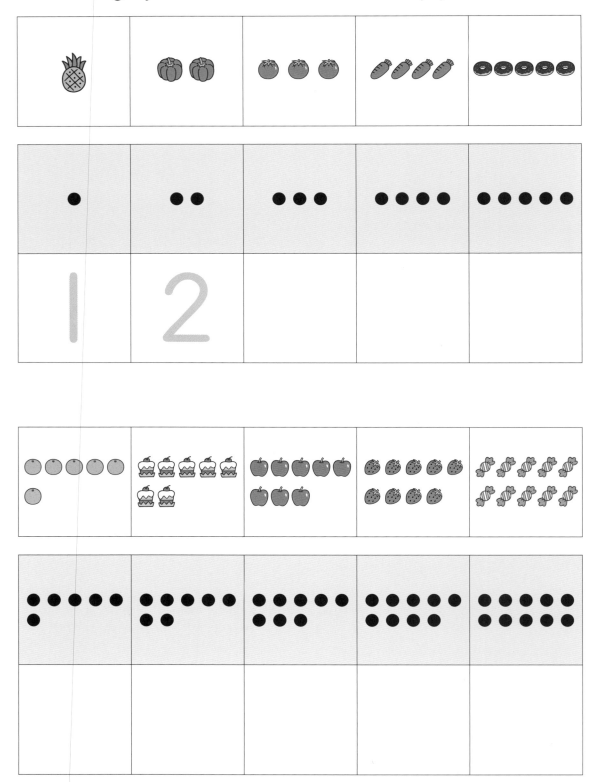

Name

Date

■How many dots (●) are there? Write the number in each box.

●	● ●	● ● ●	● ● ● ●	● ● ● ● ●
1	2	3	4	5

● ● ● ● ● ●	● ● ● ● ● ● ●	● ● ● ● ● ● ● ●	● ● ● ● ● ● ● ● ●	● ● ● ● ● ● ● ● ● ●
6	7	8	9	10

●	● ●	● ● ●	● ● ● ●	● ● ● ● ●

● ● ● ● ● ●	● ● ● ● ● ● ●	● ● ● ● ● ● ● ●	● ● ● ● ● ● ● ● ●	● ● ● ● ● ● ● ● ● ●

■How many dots (●) are there? Write the number in each box.

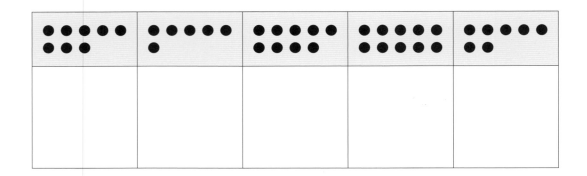

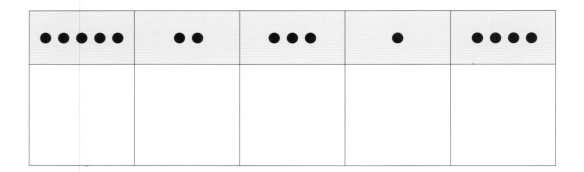

Numbers 1 to 20

Name

Date

To parents
When your child writes the numbers well, praise him or her.

■Trace the gray numbers. Then fill in the missing numbers. Say each number aloud.

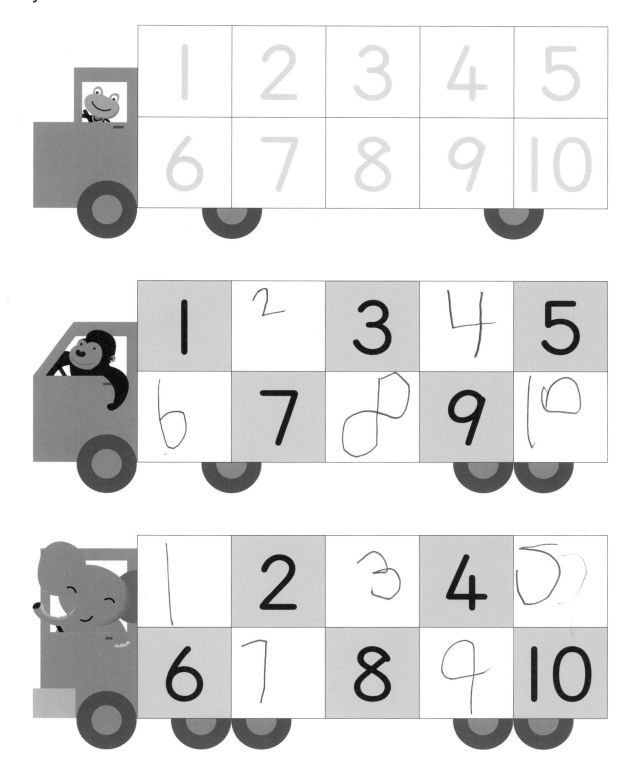

■ Trace the gray numbers and fill in the missing numbers.
Say each number aloud.

1	2	3	4	5
6	7	8	9	10
11	12	13	14	15
16	17	18	19	20

1	2	3	4	5
6	7	8	9	10
11	12	13	14	15
16	17	18	19	20

Name

Date

▪Draw a line from 1 to 20 in order while saying each number.

Hot-Air Balloon

■Draw a line from I to 20 in order while saying each number.

Number Puzzle 1 to 20
Which One Is Upside Down?

Name

Date

To parents
When your child finishes the exercise, talk with him or her about the things in the picture.

■ Draw a line from 1 to 20 in order while saying each number.

What Is the Monkey Doing?

▪ Draw a line from 1 to 20 in order while saying each number.

Counting 1 to 20

Name

Date

■Say the numbers aloud. Then draw a circle around 9, 10, and 11.

1	2	3	4	5
6	7	8	9	10
11	12	13	14	15
16	17	18	19	20

■Say the numbers aloud. Then draw a circle around 12, 13, and 14.

1	2	3	4	5
6	7	8	9	10
11	12	13	14	15
16	17	18	19	20

25 Counting 1 to 20

Name

Date

■Say the numbers aloud. Then draw a circle around 15, 16, and 17.

1	2	3	4	5
6	7	8	9	10
11	12	13	14	(15)
(16)	(17)	18	19	20

■Say the numbers aloud. Then draw a circle around 18, 19, and 20.

1	2	3	4	5
6	7	8	9	10
11	12	13	14	15
16	17	18	19	20

Writing Numbers 11 to 20

Name

Date

To parents
Tell your child the following. From 11 to 19, the number in the "ones" part increases by 1, but the number in the "tens" part does not change. When 19 increases by 1 to 20, the number in the "tens" part changes from 1 to 2, and the number in the "ones" part becomes 0.

■Trace the gray numbers and say them aloud.

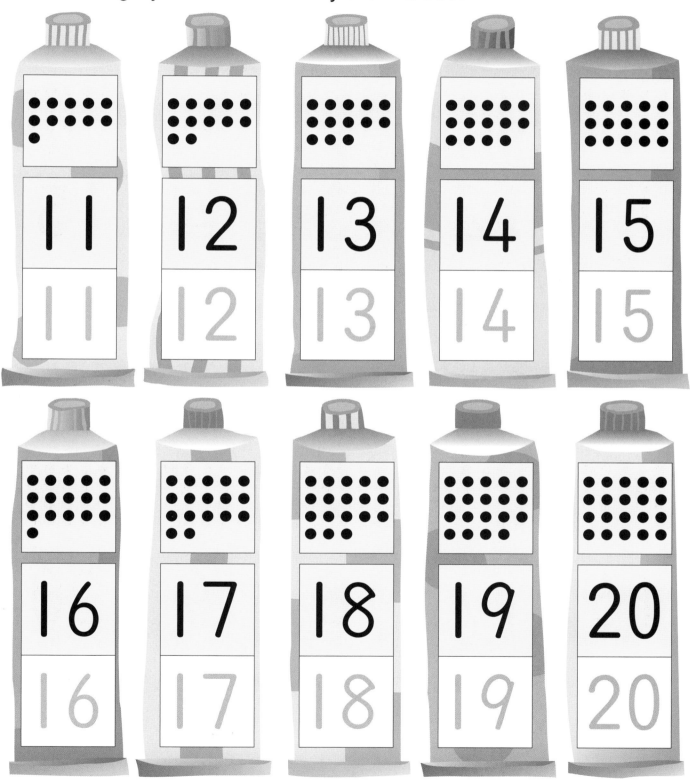

■Write the numbers and say them aloud.

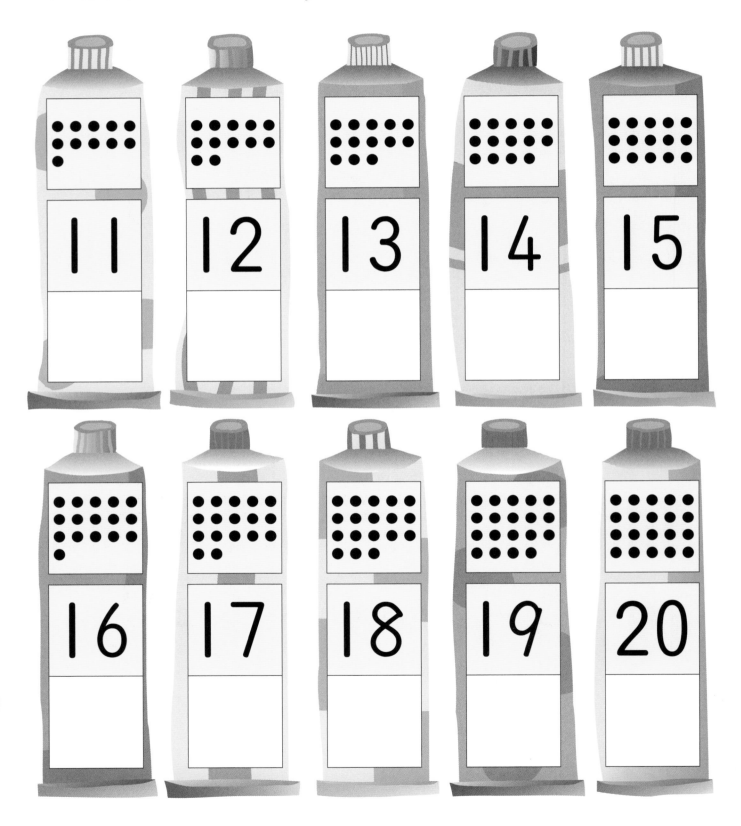

How Many? 11 to 20

■How many dots (●) are there? Trace the gray numbers.

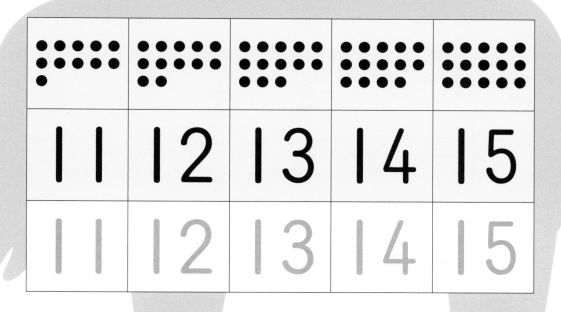

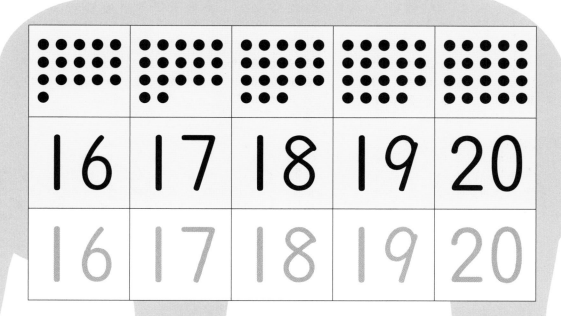

■How many dots (●) are there? Trace the gray numbers and fill in the empty boxes.

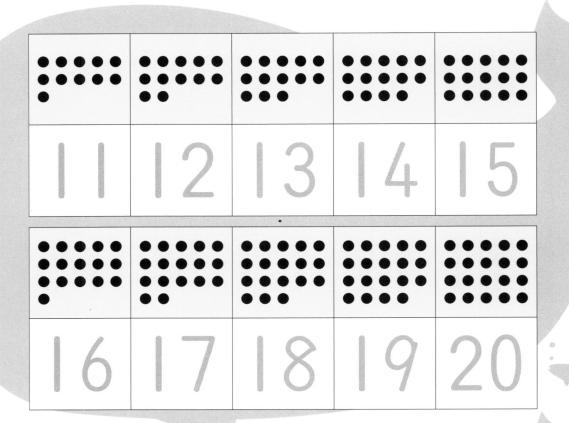

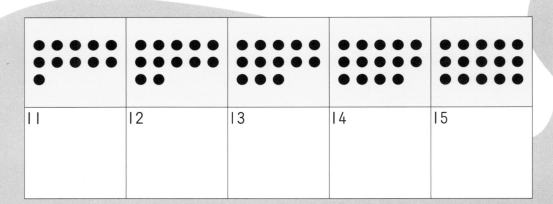

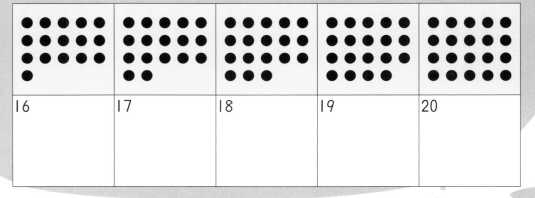

28 How Many? 6 to 15

■How many dots (●) are there? Write the number in each box.

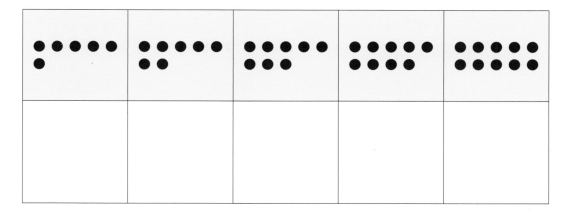

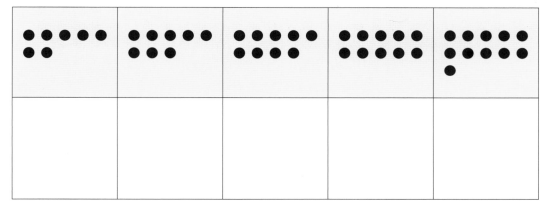

How many dots (●) are there? Write the number in each box.

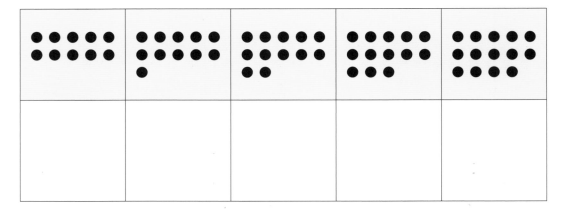

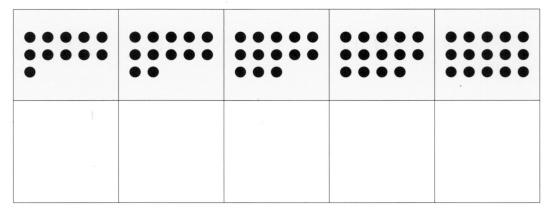

Numbers 11 to 30

Name

Date

■Trace the gray numbers. Then fill in the missing numbers.
  Say each number aloud.

■Trace the gray numbers and fill in the missing numbers.
 Say each number aloud.

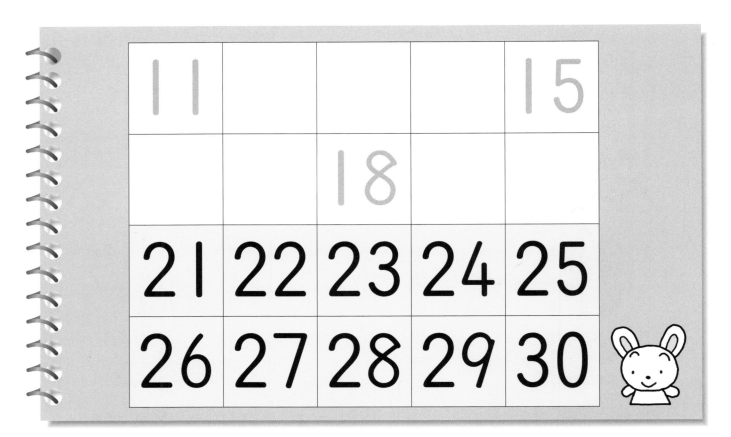

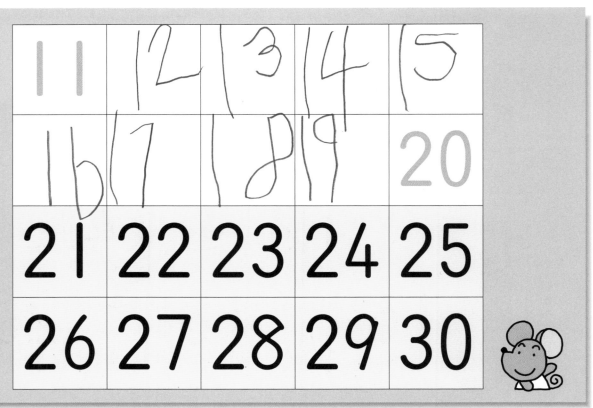

30 Number Puzzle 1 to 30
Crab

Name

Date

■Draw a line from I to 30 in order while saying each number.

Lion

■Draw a line from I to 30 in order while saying each number.

Number Puzzle 1 to 30
Let's Have Lunch!

Name

Date

To parents
When your child finishes the exercise, talk with him or her about the things in the picture.

■ Draw a line from 1 to 30 in order while saying each number.

Jack-in-the-Box

■Draw a line from 1 to 30 in order while saying each number.

32

Writing Numbers 21 to 30

Name

Date

To parents
Have your child write the numbers from 21 to 30. Do the exercise along with your child if he or she has difficulty.

■ Trace the gray numbers and say them aloud.

| 21 | 22 | 23 | 24 | 25 |
| 21 | 22 | 23 | 24 | 25 |

| 26 | 27 | 28 | 29 | 30 |
| 26 | 27 | 28 | 29 | 30 |

■Write the numbers and say them aloud.

Numbers 11 to 30

■Trace the gray numbers. Then fill in the missing numbers. Say each number aloud.

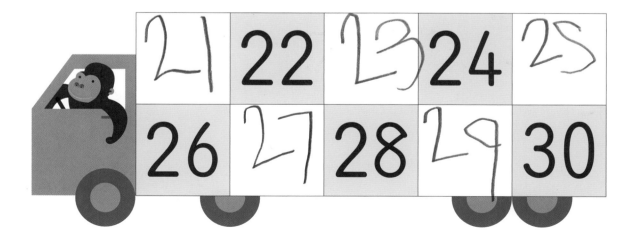

■Trace the gray numbers and fill in the missing numbers.
 Say each number aloud.

11	12	13	14	15
16	17	18	19	20
21	23	24	25	25
6	17	28	28	29

11	12	13	14	15
16	17	18	19	20
21	23	24	25	6
17	18	19	29	30

34

Review 1 to 13

Name

Date

■ Trace the gray numbers and fill in the missing numbers.
Say each number aloud.

■Trace the gray numbers and fill in the missing numbers.
 Say each number aloud.

35 Review 10 to 22

Name

Date

■ Trace the gray numbers and fill in the missing numbers.
Say each number aloud.

■Trace the gray numbers and fill in the missing numbers.
Say each number aloud.

36 Review 19 to 30

Name

Date

■Trace the gray numbers and fill in the missing numbers.
Say each number aloud.

19 20 21 22 23

20 21 22 26 24

21 22 23 24 25

22 23 24 25 26

■Trace the gray numbers and fill in the missing numbers.
Say each number aloud.

37

Review 1 to 30

Name

Date

To parents
The following pages review the numbers 1 to 30. It may be challenging for your child to finish these exercises. Specific praise will help build his or her confidence.

■ Fill in the missing numbers. Say each number aloud.

1	2	3	4	5
6	7	8	9	10
11	12	13	14	15
16	17	18	19	20
21	22	23	24	25
26	27	28	29	30

■Fill in the missing numbers. Say each number aloud.

1	2	3	4	5
6	7	8	9	10
11	12	13	14	15
16	17	18	19	20
21	22	23	24	25
26	27	28	29	30

Review 1 to 30

Name

Date

Fill in the missing numbers. Say each number aloud.

1	1	3	3	5
6	6	8	8	10
11	11	13	13	15
16	16	18	18	20
21	21	23	23	25
26	26	28	28	30

Fill in the missing numbers. Say each number aloud.

1	2	3	4	5
6	7	8	9	10
11	12	13	14	15
16	17	18	19	20
21	22	23	24	25
26	27	28	29	30

Review 1 to 30

■Fill in the missing numbers. Say each number aloud.

1	2	3	4	5
6	7	8	9	10
11	12	13	14	15
16	17	18	19	20
21	22	23	24	25
26	27	28	29	30

■Fill in the missing numbers. Say each number aloud.

				5
6				
				15
16				
				25
26				

Review 1 to 30

Name

Date

■ Write the numbers from 1 to 30.
  Say each number aloud.

■Write the numbers from 1 to 30. Say each number aloud.

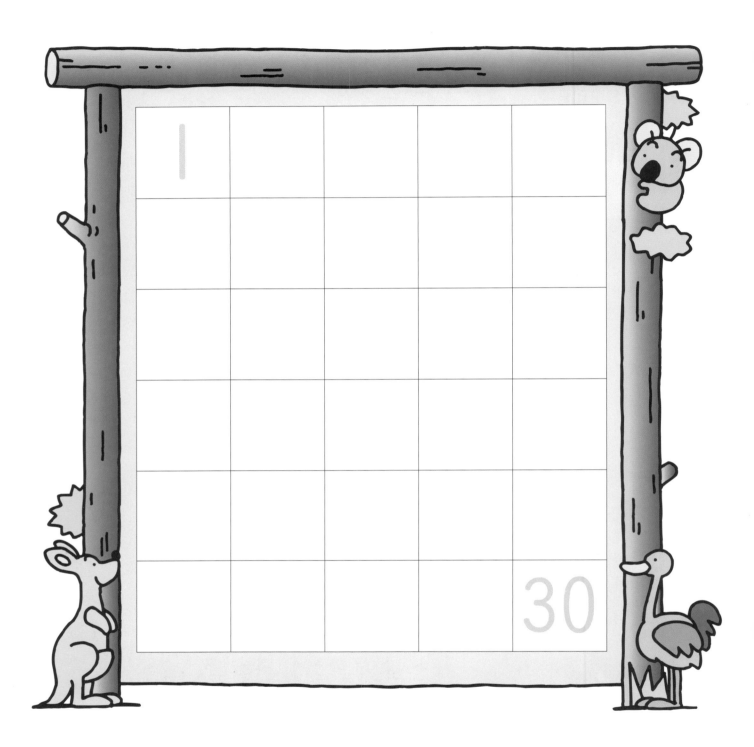

1

30

You are now able to count and write up to 30.
Congratulations!

KUM◯N

Certificate of Achievement

is hereby congratulated on completing

My Book of Numbers 1 - 30

Presented on _____ , 20 ___

_____
Parent or Guardian

0 1 2 3 4 5 6 7 8 9